NARCISSISTIC ABUSE RECOVERY

*Healing and Reclaiming Your True Self
After Narcissistic Abuse
(2023 Guide for Beginners)*

Laurence Mann

TABLE OF CONTENTS

INTRODUCTION

Consider a friend who has found their ideal partner. The partner has most of the traits anyone else hopes for in an ideal mate: confidence, attentiveness, charm, and intelligence. As a bystander,

Something may not feel quite right between the friend and their partner. Even when the conversation is directed to them, the partner may appear to be loud, dominating the conversation, or even speaking for the friend.

The attention that was noted as sweet initially seems more obsessive-based as the partner keeps track of every move the friend makes. The friend, who was once boisterous and gregarious, now appears quiet, insecure, self-conscious, and guarded, implying that they have been mistreated in some way. But without any obvious signs of abuse, no one intervenes. This is what a narcissistic, abusive relationship looks like from the outside, and why narcissists can continue their behavior.

The worst part is that the victims in these sorts of relationships are either in deep denial that the problem is within the narcissist, or they've been made to believe all fault is theirs. The situation is similar to being held in a headlock with a muzzle on and forced to stay in a completely one-sided relationship. Even when the victim musters the courage to reach out to someone, they are frequently dismissed, keeping the victim under control.

Because the very core of a person has been damaged, this type of abusive relationship is one of the most difficult to end and recover from, and it is not discriminatory in any way. It is unconcerned about people's gender, race, religion, social status, or any other classification. Narcissists and their targets can be found in all walks of life. Worse, victims believe they will never get better, which keeps them in that invisible headlock without a fight. But it doesn't have to be that way. Those who are dealing with, healing from, or recovering from the debilitating effects of being in a toxic relationship require the empowerment of information, which is the focus of this book.

Understanding the mindset of a narcissist, their personality traits, and their effects on those around them gives victims a new perspective of what they endured as well as a renewed sense of self. It's also a way to recognize warning signs in future potential relationships so that the cycle doesn't repeat itself.

This book does not cast a sympathetic light on the abuser, nor does it assist you in determining whether or not you are in this type of relationship, though you will be given some tips on how to tell if you are unsure. The emphasis is on gaining insight to strengthen your resolve to leave the relationship, the tools you need to rebuild yourself from the inside out, how to avoid being drawn back in, and how to live your new life the way you deserve to live. You are already aware that something is wrong. Your instincts are almost never wrong.

The goal is to help you get through and past the damage and rebuild your life from the inside out .and we'll walk you through every step.

CHAPTER 1

WHAT YOU REALLY WANT TO KNOW ABOUT NARCISSISTS

If you already know your partner has a narcissistic personality, you're already an expert on how difficult it can be to be in a relationship with them. Maybe you're aware of what they're about, but you can't seem to get them to leave, and they won't let you walk away. Maybe you recognize who they are and what they're doing to you, but you're not sure how to let go. Or you've managed to walk away, but you're afraid you'll either return or never find someone better. These are all valid concerns, which is why we're starting at square one with getting your life back.

The term narcissism is used so frequently that its true meaning is lost. It is most associated with people who have strong personalities and are self-assured to the point of arrogance. Those people need to be the center of attention even if the topics aren't their strong suits, and their egos influence their need to be the center of attention. Although many of these behaviors sound like those of a narcissist, there are important differences that set them apart. This will be covered in greater depth later in the chapter.

Understanding narcissists' thought processes will also be discussed. This may raise the question, "Why would I want to get into someone's head like that?" But having this knowledge definitely gives the victim an advantage. Knowing how they operate will enable you to be in control of your responses, taking away the power that they need to feel. This will not only give you the courage to leave the toxic relationship, but it will also fortify you against allowing the narcissist to entice you back.

Finally, in relation to the above point, we'll cover some possible explanations of how they became the way they are. As pointed out in the introduction, we aren't trying to give them sympathy when they have never displayed any empathy for anyone else. Knowing where they got their personality from will make you more wary of their manipulative ways or attempts to push familiar guilt buttons.

By the end of this chapter, you'll be more aware of what you've been dealing with and perhaps even feel a little more empowered.

101 on Narcissism
To some degree, most individuals display traces of narcissism occasionally. When you think about it, children are narcissistic by nature in that they expect their needs and wants to be met regardless of convenience. They, too, crave everyone's attention and work hard to obtain it. However, children quickly realize that such behavior and the level of expectation from others are not only rude but also unrealistic. They eventually grow out of it. Those who do not, and who do not learn more appropriate behavior, carry it into adulthood.

Narcissism is often misunderstood as simply having a lot of confidence in who they are, what they do, and where they want to go in life. In this sense, these individuals may simply be mentally tough with a clear path to their achievement goals, channeling their narcissistic tendencies more into ambition. The issue arises when the self becomes more important than their goals, even at the expense of other people's wants and needs. And it's at this point that it becomes a personality disorder rather than a person who is simply confident in who they are. The traits that define narcissistic personality disorder (NPD) revolve around their exaggerated sense of self-importance. Specific traits associated with the narcissistic personality individual include:

- a grandiose view of their accomplishments, talents, and capabilities; a need for constant attention and admiration, and no matter how much they receive, it never seems to be enough; a focus on superficial things (e.g., appearance, possessions, social status, etc.); and an expectation of special treatment.
- It may surprise you to learn that those with narcissistic personalities are actually insecure to the point of self-loathing, which is why they work so hard for attention.
- And it's possible that they treat others as inferior because that's how they see themselves. Under the umbrella of narcissism, there are four main categories that individuals can be specifically grouped into based on what their foci are.

The characteristics listed above can be found in all types of narcissism. The main distinction between these is how they express personality traits.

1. **Stereotypical:** This group consists of stereotypical narcissists who openly and unapologetically exhibit the personality traits. They don't see how their behavior is wrong or hurtful and will actually point the finger elsewhere, deflecting all blame or wrongdoing onto others.

2. **Vulnerable:** These people are also referred to as "closet narcissists" because, while they still believe in their superiority, they are more introverted and avoid the spotlight. Rather than actively seeking special treatment, they usually attach themselves to those who are popular and already receive it. They gain attention by portraying themselves as victims or by displaying false generosity. In other words, they don't give from the heart because they want attention.

3. **Communal:** This one is a little harder to spot until you look closely at the person. These individuals appear to be strong advocates in the community or with specific charities, but, they are not supporting a cause for humanitarian reasons but rather for praise and recognition. einsteineruploaded with.

4. **Malignant:** Of all the main types of narcissists, this is the most toxic and ruthless. These people are highly manipulative and appear to enjoy exploiting others.

This group is aggressive, controlling, and deceptive, and they will go to any length to dominate. Worse yet, they have no remorse for anything they do. Under each of these main categories, there are a few subtypes of narcissists depending on how their actions are viewed or experienced by others. Here is a list of the subtypes:

1. **Open:** This group employs methods that are clearly visible to all. The traditional and communal groups are always visible.

2. **Covert:** Because these narcissists are so good at concealing their actions, it is difficult for those in relationships with them to persuade others of the truth. They use a sneaky and passive-

aggressive approach to manipulate others without their knowledge at first. The vulnerable population is always hidden. Because of the very nature of what they do and their high lack of empathy and remorse, those in the communal group can be either overt or covert.

3. **cerebral:** The name implies brain function, but people in this group regard their intellect as superior, leading them to believe they are smarter than everyone else. They dominate the conversation, constantly demonstrating their knowledge, and interrupt when others try to speak.

4. **Somatic:** People in this group are preoccupied with their bodies and judge others based on their outward appearance. They are very likely to seek partners who can serve as "shiny objects" to increase their visibility and popularity. They obsess over their weight, physique, and appearance and will criticize their partner—or others—for failing to meet their expectations. People in these categories can be classified as belonging to any of the four major groups.

5. **Inverted**: only applies to vulnerable or covert groups. These are the wounded victims who

blame everyone else for what has happened to them. They associate with other narcissists in order to feel exceptional, and these people are most likely to have developed their personality as a result of childhood trauma.

6. **Sadistic:** These people fall squarely into the malignant main category. This subtype is like sociopathic or psychopathic mindsets in that they take great pleasure in other people's suffering. They thrive on humiliating, injuring, and destroying other people's self-worth, and this mentality can even permeate their sexual practices.

7. **Spiritual:** These individuals tend to display a "holier than thou" mindset and use religion and spirituality to shame others or justify their treatment of others It is clear that narcissists exhibit characteristics from each of these individual categories, but their focus is sometimes narrowed to one area based on what is most important to them.

How Do Narcissists Develop Their Personality?

There does not appear to be a solid, proven reason why some people develop narcissistic personalities while others do not. There are some genetic and environmental influences, but nothing absolute. Studies of the brain areas responsible for emotion processing, empathy, and certain cognitive functions have revealed some deterioration or lack of development in those with this personality disorder (Payco, 2022). We are not born with personality disorders, but they develop in childhood because of experience, genes, and what they are exposed to in each of their environments (e.g., school, friends, family, etc.). It's important to remember that just because a young person exhibits certain narcissistic characteristics doesn't mean they'll develop a disorder. It could be age-related characteristics (for example, self-focus). Keeping these points in mind, here are a few other reasons why narcissists develop the way they do:

- Developing an insensitive temperament at a young age
- Taking on manipulative behaviors from caregivers, siblings, or friends
- Being overly praised for good behavior while being severely chastised for bad behavior
- Uncertain expectations or boundaries
- Unreasonably praised.
- Childhood experiences of trauma, neglect, abandonment, or abuse
- Caregiving that is inconsistent or unreliable
- Growing up, they were heavily overindulged by those around them.
- unrealistic emphasis on appearance, body image, or capabilities

You now have a clear definition of narcissism, as well as their personality traits and possible reasons for developing their undesirable personality traits. The following chapter will focus on the tactics narcissists use to maintain control over others (particularly those with whom they have intimate relationships), as well as important points to remember when dealing with them.

CHAPTER 2

THE NARCISSIST'S TACTICS TO CONTROL

Understanding the narcissist's personality is important so that those closest to them understand what they're dealing with. Those who have dealt with toxic behavior for a long enough period of time will have a deeper level of understanding that will help protect them from further harm. Those who are new to a relationship with such a person now have solid information to either risk moving forward with their new partner or to remove themselves before getting too involved.

Deep research on the narcissist in your life may appear to be counterproductive in some ways. Don't we seem to be doing exactly what they want? Isn't it true that they want our undivided attention? On the surface, it may feel that way, but, first, they don't know you're gathering information for your benefit unless you tell them. Second, you're not doing what they expect of you because the information you're receiving is to get away from them and heal from their abuse, not to inflate their ego.

Using that as a starting point, this chapter will look at the different ways narcissists try to control you. Again, while the terms themselves may be unfamiliar, their definitions may be. Recognize these tactics, name them, and put a stop to them It's easy to fall victim to their tactics, as well as to be drawn back into them once you've had the courage to end the relationship. Once you know what they are doing, you need to be strong on the inside, so you know how to respond. Narcissists continue to engage in toxic behavior because they are permitted to do so. When confronted with someone who will not succumb to their charms but also understands how to fight them, the narcissist will retreat. They'll quickly lose interest in someone who requires too much effort to attract their attention.

However, an important side note should be made. Although most narcissists won't waste their time with someone they can't control, sadistic narcissists are less likely to let go as easily as others. This group is more likely to stalk, make the victim look like the bad guy, or attack the victim's good nature or reputation just to twist the knife of pain. Remember that they derive a lot of pleasure from another person's suffering, so any retaliation on the victim's part will not be tolerated. But don't give up. There is both light and safety. In the chapter's conclusion, we'll discuss whether the narcissist can change and when to accept that they won't. This is a tough realization because it also means accepting that you are a victim of abuse, and the next chapter will guide you through that.

Dysfunctional Narcissist Coping Mechanisms
This chapter begins with the various controlling methods used by a narcissist to protect their valuable ego. They do this by using a wide range of unhealthy ways to attract, keep, and control their partners or other people they let close to them. If victims do not notice these methods at first, they should do so as soon as the narcissist's spell begins to wear off. Once the victim recognizes and labels these methods, they can use the suggestions in this book not only to control their reactions but also to shift blame back onto the narcissist. Understand that recognizing the tactics is easier than responding to them effectively at first. If one isn't strong enough to fight back at first, it's critical to be consciously aware of what's going on. This is the first

and most important step in discontinuing the toxic treatment from which you will draw during your healing process The narcissist's most common tactics for maintaining control are as follows:

- **Using love-bombing:** Before the narcissist can even get close enough to pull any tricks, they have to get the person of their focus to trust them. Love-bombing may appear innocent and flattering at first but be wary. The idea is to overwhelm the bomber with gifts, surprises, and other signs of affection in order to pique his interest in wanting to spend more time with him. It may not be obvious to the recipient at first, but these are acts of manipulation to gain trust. So, how can the recipient tell when the intentions are genuine and when they are being manipulated by a narcissist? They are watching how you react in your world and then showering you with attention and gifts based on what makes you the happiest. But all of this affection comes at a high price. This is how the recipient should perceive love-bombing:

    - Things are moving far too quickly for comfort. A relationship takes time, but it should be concerning when someone mentions love, having a family, and marriage not long after meeting.
    - The bomber will appear extreme and over-the-top in their approach, always telling you what you want to hear, even about your insecurities, with no sense of genuineness.
    - If they believe you are not responding positively, they will take steps back until they find the appropriate response. Remember that they aren't concerned

with the sincerity of your approach, only with how you appear.

- The fact that they may be very nice to you but not to others is a major indicator. Many victims miss this because they enjoy the attention, but it should be a warning sign that they will be treated similarly before long.
- They'll start asking you probing questions about any difficult times you've been through, and they'll really push for you to be honest.
- This is another major red flag because such things should arise naturally after strong, mutual trust has been established. The narcissist is just pocketing ammunition for future use.

- **Gaslighting:** This tactic is felt before the recipient realizes what is happening to them. This is one of the most severe forms of manipulation, leaving the victim befuddled and questioning their own sanity. When this happens for a long enough period, the victim loses their ability to trust themselves or their perceptions of what is real. And, once again, there are various ways for a toxic person to deceive someone:

  - They tell you that you're not remembering something correctly or that you're simply incorrect when you know you're correct.
  - They make you believe that your thoughts and feelings are unimportant to anyone else.
  - They withhold information and then act as if they don't understand what you're saying.

- They are giving you the silent treatment.
    - They cause you to question the validity of your own thoughts.
    - They justify their actions by claiming that they are for your own good.
    - They deny that anything happened.

- **Projection** is the act of one person projecting unpleasant feelings or accountability onto another. A narcissist will not accept responsibility for their actions and will go out of their way to make someone else take the blame in extremely damaging and cruel ways.
- **Deflection:** Anyone who has tried to win an argument with a narcissist is familiar with this tactic. This is the act of talking around an issue or problem until the original subject matter is lost or forgotten. Have you ever left a conversation feeling lost, confused, or unsure of what point you were trying to make in the first place? To avoid accountability, the narcissist deflected the conversation.
- **Distortion:** This is a tactic in which the narcissist twists the truth so that you doubt yourself, even though the facts were clear in your mind prior to confronting the narcissist. They are experts at lying and use several tricks to change your reality:

    - They are constantly attempting to establish their superiority.
    - They draw a conclusion based on one incident and generalize it to everything else.
    - They draw conclusions based on their feelings rather than facts.

- They will either exaggerate the significance of specific details or minimize or completely disregard them.
  - They often put unrealistic obligations on others using "should' statements.
  - They play the victim even when the situation has nothing to do with them.
  - They play the emotional card, obscuring any sense of logical reasoning, if a few others, if a few others, if a few.
- **Triangulation:**When a narcissist gets someone else to help them hurt their victim, this is called triangulation. "This is most often done as a form of punishment for the victim, either for failing to do what is expected of them or for finally seeing the light and ending the toxic relationship.
- **Splitting**: is a type of black-and-white thinking in which there are no other options.
- **Negging:** is a type of emotional manipulation in which the person gives backhanded compliments to elicit self-doubt and gradually erode the receiver's self-esteem.

These strategies are sometimes used so subtly that the target person isn't even aware it's happening until they're well into it. Even so, one should be able to sense that something isn't right based on how they feel. Gut feelings are extremely powerful and almost never wrong.

Dos and Don'ts of Reacting to a Narcissist
Following the discussion in this chapter, it is clear that communicating with them is difficult. a goal of achieving a goal of achieving You now have the advantage of understanding not only what to look out for in terms of their personality but also how they carry out their

mission of controlling what happens in their environment.

This section will delve a little deeper into the "must-knows" to have on your side. We'll go over ten don'ts when dealing with a narcissist and why they're important to know. This empowers the victim to stop them in their tracks and keep them at bay. We'll wrap up the chapter with seven dos and don'ts when dealing with a narcissist, as well as how to end the argument before they try one of their tactics.

First, here are some general dos and don'ts when dealing with a narcissist:

1. **Never undervalue them.** This is a group of people who are never content on any level. It's clear that they've developed a strong sense of self that no other person can match, let alone surpass. That being said, they know exactly what to say to get what they want. Keep an eye on them and question everything they say, especially hints of willingness to change.
2. **There will be no empathy**. One of the defining characteristics of a narcissistic personality is a lack of empathy. To feel empathy, a person must be willing to see a situation through the eyes of another person and understand that other people are deserving of and deserve compassion. What a narcissist cannot give is what they do not feel. Rather than trying to persuade them, concentrate on honoring and respecting yourself by staying within your boundaries (this will be covered in greater detail in a later chapter).
3. **Never ever give them ammunition**. Take care with your thoughts, feelings, and other aspects of your inner self. Anything you tell them will be used against you in some way.

4. **There's more to them than meets the eye.** Narcissists work hard to maintain the appearance of perfection and superiority. The irony is that underneath all the masks, they feel exactly the opposite of the image they portray. We can feel compassion for them as fellow humans, but we must not be duped by their tactics.

5. **Put on your best poker face.** A narcissist views everyone as an enemy or someone to exploit, and they save their worst behavior for those they allow to be closest to them. Never give them the satisfaction of knowing they got to you, no matter what they say or do. That is their main goal; don't make it easier for them.

6. **Don't count on their help.** Narcissists have no loyalty to others. If a person fails to meet their needs or desires, they are discarded. Expecting this from someone who is only interested in themselves is a recipe for disaster.

7. **You owe no explanations or justifications to them.** They owe this to their victims, but it should not be expected. Attempting to explain or justify feelings to a narcissist is another way to provide them with ammunition. They refuse to communicate, will not reason, and are uninterested in resolving issues. They are only concerned with winning.

8. **Never minimize or downplay their behavior.** As an extension of the preceding point, just because you can't get them to listen to how their words, actions, and behavior hurt you doesn't mean you should keep it to yourself. It's critical that you console yourself with the knowledge that they have no right to make others feel that way and that you will not let their afflictions get under your skin. Your self-esteem is precious and valuable, and it should not be harmed.

9. **Expect no accountability.** This has already been mentioned but understanding that they will not accept responsibility for their actions saves a lot of time and energy. It is certainly appropriate to verbalize their responsibility for their actions for your own peace of mind. But don't expect them to take what you say seriously.
10. **Don't try to exact revenge.** It's not worth the effort to beat them at their own game or to avenge yourself. The narcissist has spent their entire life doing what they do, and they are experts in the field of pain and hurt. Going up against them at their own game is like a lightweight boxer going up against the heavyweight world champion. The best way to fight back in your own way is to stay true to yourself and your values.

Some of the don'ts may seem obvious, but for those who are tangled right in the middle of a narcissist's web or who are new in this sort of relationship, it's imperative to stay informed and protect themselves. The dos are intended to assist you with the subject focus in the following chapter. The emphasis will be on recognizing the impact of narcissistic abuse on overall health. Those who witness what is happening to them will find it easier to confront the abuser and find the strength to flee. For those who are still unsure, the information will hopefully lead to realization and acceptance. Nothing is more important than your health, and you won't be able to function for long if it is compromised.

These tips will give you the courage you need to confront the narcissistic abuser. The manipulation will continue even after they realize their tactics will no longer keep you alive, so stay strong.

Here are some things to avoid when confronted by a narcissist:

- **Let go of blame**. As you know by now, trying to make the narcissist take responsibility for their part in things going wrong is a waste of energy and emotion. They will not admit to anything that makes them appear to be the polar opposite of the perfect person they believe they are.
- **Empathize with their emotions.** "Why should I give them a shred of empathy when they have none for anyone else?" many people may think. Sometimes relating to their feelings is the best way to end an argument quickly, or at least deflate it.
- **Let them think you're in it together.** This may be difficult to implement, but they will respond better to a gentler approach. Allow them to believe you're all in this together. Using 'I' or 'you' language singles out each of you, which is never a good thing with a narcissist, so using 'we' language is a wise move. They'll be angry enough that you've confronted them or even defended yourself but using 'we' reminds them that your actions involve both of you.
- **Prioritize yourself**. This is difficult to put into practice when you've been forced to prioritize someone else's wants and needs over your own. Keep yourself in front of them and don't give them the power to bring you back into their web.
- **Ignore the bait.** When confronted, the narcissist will attempt to turn everything around on you, using insults, blame, or belittling. Of course, a natural reaction is to jump into defense mode, but that's exactly what they want. Ignore the

insults, tune out the bait, and keep your attention on the main issue.

- **It's okay not to get an apology.** We've already discussed that they don't feel remorse or empathy, both of which you need to feel to offer a sincere apology. Simply put, they can't offer something to which they don't feel or relate.
- **When all else fails, feed their ego**. If you can't find your breakaway in any of these scenarios, master the art of distraction. They enjoy talking about themselves and being given the opportunity to demonstrate that they know more than anyone else. If changing the subject does not work, seek their advice. This is a last-ditch effort to break the never-ending circle of argument.

The discussions will better prepare you to absorb the next chapter's focus on recognizing, dealing with, and calling out the narcissist for their abusive behavior. It's time to take the first step in halting the toxic relationship and preparing to head down the road of recovery.

CHAPTER 3

RECOGNIZING AND STOPPING NARCISSISTIC ABUSE

The most difficult aspect of being in an abusive relationship, regardless of category, is realizing you have been abused. Acceptance is essential for developing the courage to end the relationship, accepting the reconstruction of your self-worth in recovery, and maintaining the resilience to move forward in healing. Acceptance does not imply accepting what has happened to you; rather, it means becoming aware of the abuse in order to make positive changes.

This chapter will be the book's high point. Armed with information about the narcissist—their personality and tactics—it will be easier to begin turning the tables. It's critical for victims of a narcissist's venomous ways to understand that the treatment they're receiving isn't normal, they don't deserve it, and it does more than just make them feel bad about themselves (which is enough). Abuse is harmful to your overall health, especially when it affects every aspect of your well-being. It can have long-term psychological consequences, including trauma from which you may never fully recover. Finally, because abuse damages the very core of your being and your self-worth, it may take a long time to trust or even see yourself in the same light.

Should one person be given so much power that they can destroy another being? No, we say! And so will you. This chapter will help you become conscious of how deeply the narcissist's abuse has harmed you. You'll be able to spot the warning signs and respond with more positive responses. You'll figure out how to confront your abuser and then cut ties with them. And, just in case you need some extra motivation, we'll go over exactly how that person has interfered with your overall functioning. It's time to realign the disjointed parts of your mind, body, and spirit selves, which begins with reclaiming the power the abuser believes they have over you Some of you may find this a difficult topic to discuss. To get through certain points, especially those focusing on physical or mental health, it may be a good idea to contact your primary healthcare provider. Knowing that both areas have been through a lot, having some insight and care to make sure you come out on top is a wise choice.

Finally Recognizing the Light
All types of abuse tend to follow a consistent and predictable pattern that stems from and revolves around control. The narcissist begins slowly and steadily to draw their target in, then showers the person with attention and shiny things to get the target where they want them before revealing their true self. It should be noted here that narcissistic personalities and abuse are not always associated. Even though they can be controlling and manipulative, not all abusers have narcissistic personalities. People can have some of the characteristics of a narcissist without being abusive. That being said, it does not give anyone the right to cause harm to others for personal gain. And here are the main indicators that you're in a narcissistic relationship:

1. **They were perfect at first**. We've talked about it before, but it bears repeating. A narcissist wants you to believe they adore you and place you on a pedestal. Once they have you, they stop

trying as hard, and you end up having to work harder to keep them.

2. **Others do not see the narcissist in the same way that you do**. It's difficult enough to see it yourself, but when those around you, particularly their friends and family, make excuses for them, you begin to doubt yourself even more. Maintain your focus on what you see.

3. **They are slandering you.** They make you appear to be a bad person in order to maintain their perfect façade Typically, this entails spreading rumors, criticizing you behind your back, or fabricating lies about you. The worst part is that when you try to correct the situation or assign blame where it belongs, the narcissist uses your defense to support their own lies. It's frustrating because the generous, wonderful person they were initially is still what those around you see, even if you see them for who they truly are.

4. **You are experiencing anxiety and/or depression symptoms.** The toxic person may have made you worry about them not acting as expected or about them not doing something right or well enough. You may have lost sleep, lost interest in things you used to enjoy, or developed a "What's the point?" attitude because of making this person your entire world. You basically absorb all the negative talk and treatment and believe it all.This is a dangerous mindset to be in, so seek outside help as soon as possible if you believe you are heading down this path.

5. **You suffer from unexplained physical ailments.** It's not surprising that when you internalize a lot of negativities, you start to feel sick. Changes in appetite, stomach issues, body aches, insomnia, and fatigue are some common

symptoms that aren't related to any ongoing condition. These are normal stress responses, but if they worsen or become chronic, see a doctor as soon as possible.

6. **You are feeling isolated**. This is another common symptom of abuse. If something is seriously wrong, the narcissist may have isolated you from friends or family, either through their own actions or by convincing you that no one cares about you.

7. **You become paralyzed**. You freeze when you emotionally remove yourself from the abuse. It's a coping mechanism for lessening the severity of your treatment by numbing the pain.

8. **You don't believe in yourself, even when making simple decisions.** It's not surprising that you can't make decisions when criticism and devaluation have destroyed your self-esteem. If you're also being gaslighted, you'll have even more reason to doubt yourself.

9. **You can't set limits.** The narcissist lacks them and does not respect them, which makes it difficult to keep them away even after you've managed to flee. Setting boundaries will be covered in greater detail in a later chapter.

10. **You've lost touch with your true self**. The person you become when you are involved with a narcissistic abuser is not the person you were before you became involved with them. They've molded you into the person they want you to be, leaving you feeling lost and insecure with no true sense of purpose.

11. **You never feel like you're doing anything correctly.** We mentioned it briefly above, but this is one of the most common signs of narcissistic abuse. In the grand scheme of things, you may be constantly blamed when things go wrong, even when it isn't your fault. You may do

something exactly as they instruct, but they will still find fault with the outcome. It's similar to how a private feels when he or she is unsure whether or not the Drill Sergeant will find something wrong with their efforts.

12. **You're walking on eggshells.** This happens when you try to avoid conflict, maltreatment, or backlash by going above and beyond to please the abuser.

This list of warning signs shows that ignoring what a narcissistic abuser is doing to you can have long-term mental, physical, and emotional consequences. To say the least, that isn't fair, and no one should ever feel the need to exert control over another. So, what can you do to prevent the train from reaching its final destination? We discussed how to reduce the intensity of an argument in the previous chapter. Now we'll go over five strategies for confronting the narcissist about their abuse and emerging relatively unscathed.

These are some skills to have to create and strengthen boundaries:

1. **Inform them**. To put it bluntly, narcissists have poor interpersonal and communication skills. Use incentives or other motivators to get them to think about how their actions affect others. They may not empathize with or appear to understand what you're saying, but at least you can say you tried to see it from your perspective.

2. **Be aware of your personal rights**. It is critical to understand your rights to demand that you be treated fairly and with respect. You have the right to say no; you have the right to your feelings; and you have the right to privacy, and there are no wedding or relationship vows that state you are at the beck and call of your partner. When a person has been abused for a long period

of time, they may lack the confidence or self-esteem to assert their rights. The more power they reclaim, however, the less power the abuser has.

3. **Be confident.** This is something that requires confidence and practice, but it is well worth it. Being assertive means standing up for yourself and being proud of your identity.

4. **Implement your strategies.** You have an advantage because you are aware of your wants, what the narcissist demands, what you can do, and those secret, tiny areas over which you may have power. Utilize these resources to develop your own strategies.

5. **Re-establish your boundaries**. A boundary is a line in the sand that cannot be seen. It determines the point at which you will not allow others to cross, or they will harm you. These are non-negotiable, and everyone else must be aware of and respect them. However, before you can make those lines clear to others, you must first understand them.

6. **Be prepared to face the consequences.** As an extension of the preceding point, if someone attempts to disregard your boundaries, make sure you punish them. There is no need for a threat, just a statement like, "If you _______, we can't hang out, date, talk, etc." You're just telling them that stepping over the line hurts you, and if they choose to ignore that, you won't put up with it.

The narcissist will not tolerate you defending yourself, but it is still necessary. Advocating for yourself will boost your self-esteem, confidence, and self-worth. You'll then be ready to recover and heal.

The Health Consequences of Narcissistic Abuse

Several of the consequences of narcissistic abuse were discussed in the symptoms section above. This section will go over some additional and specific effects of this abuse on your overall health The effects of narcissistic abuse can vary depending on how long the victim was exposed to it and how severe the abuse was. Here are some other ways that this type of abuse can harm your health:

- **Self-destructive behavior:** When someone has been in a controlling relationship for a long enough time, they continue to feel shame and guilt even after the relationship has ended. This can lead to self-harm and substance abuse in order to cope with what the abuser has done to them.
- **Overly obliging:** Being forced to prioritize the needs and desires of another person from the moment you wake up until you go to bed can lead to you extending the people-pleasing into other areas of your life.
- **Trust issues:** Being mentally abused to the point where a person doubts or does not trust themselves or others can result in severe trust issues. This can even lead to more serious issues, like social anxiety. It fosters skepticism about what others say, what they truly mean, and their sincerity.
- **Emotionally disconnected:** It is not uncommon for people to be unsure of how to respond emotionally to situations or people, or to express any emotions at all.
- **Cognitive problems** can be caused by the bad treatment or by physical symptoms that make the person sick. Lack of sleep can lead to a lot of the problems we've already talked about, as well as digestive problems. Memory loss, an inability

to concentrate, losing focus while performing basic tasks, or "spacing out" are also concerns.

- **Can't forgive yourself:** Feelings of not being good enough, shame, and blame fade over time, but they never go away completely. Like PTSD, one minor trigger can be enough to relive the trauma. Another aspect of this is damaged self-worth, which causes us to make little effort to achieve our goals or dreams or to self-sabotage because we believe we don't deserve happiness or success.

Recognizing that everything you've been through is abuse and informing yourself about the effects it's had on your health is a good thing. Yes, it's difficult to see how much the abuse has hurt you on the inside. It should also inspire you to know that you have the control and power to stop it, change your life, and look forward to a better future That is the focus of our next chapter, which will lead you to the first steps on your road to recovery.

STOP
BULLYING

CHAPTER 4

RECOVERING FROM NARCISSISTIC ABUSE

After reading the last chapter, you should feel more motivated to take the steps you need to get away from your toxic partner. If you've already decided to leave or convinced them to, you've already taken the first baby step toward recovery and healing. If you haven't already relocated, we'll give you some pointers on how to do so as quickly and painlessly as possible. It's time to start living your life the way you deserve Once you've decided to leave your abuser, this chapter has a lot of tips to help you get back on your feet. You don't have to keep thinking that no one will believe you, help you, or even be there for you. Yes, there will be those who support the narcissist, but only because they are skilled at sabotage, and not all witnesses are so easily swayed.

The next step is to plan for getting better, which should include a strong network of people who can help you. Not only will you have tools and strategies to help you prepare for your recovery journey, but you'll also have a plan in place for when your abuser enters your thoughts and triggers emotions. Getting over an abusive relationship involves the same part of your brain that oversees keeping substance addictions at bay. Because the narcissist was your bad habit that took over your life and hurt you, it will take inner strength, perseverance, and willpower to resist their charms. We'll start with a few important things you might not have expected to happen while going through narcissist abuse recovery. This will be a strong pull to take you into the next chapter's focus on inner self-healing.

How to Get Away from a Narcissist

Ending a toxic relationship with a narcissist is difficult enough, but actually picking up and leaving that person will be one of the most difficult decisions you will face— but it will also be one of the best and healthiest decisions you will ever make. However, you will find it much easier to let go than the narcissist, who will not make it easy. Indeed, you may have some serious doubts about whether you're making the right choice. If there is a child involved, second thoughts about leaving may become even more intense. The most important question you should ask yourself, which isn't even on this short list, is whether you want your child to continue witnessing the toxic person's abusive behavior towards you. More importantly, do you want that person to have the same influence on your child? Hopefully, you answered "no" to both of those questions.

Before we remind you of the reasons, you're better off without them, consider the following:

- **What if I give them a second chance? Is it conceivable?** Anything is possible in terms of humanitarian response. In the case of narcissists, however, the answer is no. They see nothing wrong with their behavior and blame you for any wrongdoing, and their treatment of you deteriorates as you stay in the relationship. That should be the strong, lengthy response you require to stick to your decision.
- **What if they try to call or text me?** They will because they dislike losing. Sticking to a strict "no contact" rule, which we'll discuss later, is the best way to handle their attempts at contact.

This is a rule you must enforce, and you cannot leave the door open for them.

- **Is it possible to co-parent with a narcissist**? This is a difficult question that may require the assistance of a therapist to work through with both parents. To begin, parenting is about cooperation and collaboration in all decisions concerning the child's care. When one parent is unable to perform these duties, the situation may necessitate some intervention. After all, the child in such a case is not an object to be fought over; they are a young person whose rights, needs, and care should be met. If the narcissist is unwilling or unable to cooperate, do what is best for the child first and foremost.

- **How can I keep a narcissist from influencing or harming my child?** Whether they are a friend, relative, parent, teacher, or someone else, the people around children have a big impact on them. If there are any indications that the child is being mistreated in the same way that you have, intervene immediately. Talk to your child about the importance of negotiation and fair treatment. Allow no abuse around them, and do not lower yourself to the level of the abuser by insulting, putting them down, or otherwise openly expressing negative feelings. If you show your child the best, non-conflictive behavior when dealing with others, even when influenced by the narcissist, you are teaching them how to deal with adversity. It may not appear so at first, but they notice and appreciate what you're doing. They will look up to you in the future for handling situations with grace.

- **What should I do if the narcissistic parent is awarded custody of my child**? This could happen, as difficult as it is to believe. As the estranged parent, all you can do is make sure the child isn't being manipulated, used to hurt you, or otherwise mistreated. Try to remind yourself that the situation is not your fault and try to live the best life possible. Maintain open lines of communication with your child and listen to them with empathy when you speak with them. This is something they might not get from the other caregiver. Under no circumstances should you tolerate or complain about your child's abuse or disrespect. Make time for self-care (which will be covered in greater detail in a later chapter) and surround yourself with loving, caring, and supportive people. Above all, never give up hope. Don't go a day without telling your child how much you love them.

Recovering from a toxic relationship does not entail blaming the abuser entirely. It's more about dealing with the feelings that initially drew you to the person. It also entails fully recognizing the 'you' who was pushed aside during the relationship. That means you have to look past the pain the person caused and deal with the cause of the pain. It's critical at this point to remind yourself of all the reasons you're leaving. And just because that person does not intend to make your exit easy, you must remember that you are stronger than you believe. Not everyone in the same situation will trust their instincts, stand firm behind their boundaries, and forge ahead no matter how difficult it appears. In addition, here are a few things to keep in mind to ensure that your getaway goes as smoothly as possible:

1. **There will be no more chances.** You'd think that someone who treated you unworthy of their company would have no problem letting you go, right? Wrong. In fact, they may initially beg you to stay, make promises to change, share their sob

stories, or even return to love-bombing you for you to change your mind. If you fall into their trap, it won't be long before they return to their old ways or treat you even worse than before to punish you. To cut a long story short, Give them no second (or third, or fourth) chances. You've made your decision; now they must live with it.

2. **Do not tell them you are leaving immediately.** This may appear to contradict what has been said previously, but delaying informing the abuser of your intention to leave may be a wise decision. In the best-case scenario, leaving when they aren't present will reduce a lot of drama, and they don't need an exact time and date of when you're planning to leave. As previously stated, the narcissist will do everything in their power to keep you, not because they care about your relationship but because you have the audacity to leave them. Protect yourself to the greatest extent possible.

3. **Don't give them the chance to spy on you.** This extends beyond simply changing the passwords on all your devices. You must also ensure that they cannot track where you are or what you are doing. Log out of everything, change your passwords, create a new email address, and check your phone for trackers. This may appear to be overkill, but it is better to be safe than sorry.

4. **Switch your bank account**. They shouldn't be able to reach you through your bank if you never shared accounts, debt, or assets with the narcissist. If you shared an account with them, remove yourself from it, close it, or simply take what's yours and open your own without them knowing.

5. **Reestablish contact with family and friends.** You might not have had contact with close

friends or family for a long time because narcissists aren't open to their partners having supportive relationships outside of their control. Some of them may have known something wasn't right but didn't know how to intervene without making matters worse. Even after a break, good friends and family will always be there for you.

6. **Remove the other toxic people**. As an extension of the preceding point, not everyone will be as enthusiastic. Indeed, they may even support the narcissist by believing their lies. Take advantage of the opportunity to get rid of the others who share the same mindset as you walk out the door on the abuser. You don't need more people like that in your life.

7. **Do not return for any reason once you have left.** We mentioned earlier that ending an abusive relationship is like breaking a habit in the brain. It is challenging to break a habit after repeatedly doing something until you do it without thinking. Consider your narcissistic abuser to be a habit that you must break, including the cravings that try to entice you back to it. It's finished; there's no reason to go back.

8. **Discard any love-bombing trinkets or gifts.** Let's take it a step further. Gather everything that reminds you of that person and throw it away. You don't need anything to remind you of their presence, and the act of throwing things away is significant. Every trace of them has vanished from your environment, allowing you to move on.

9. **Accept your trauma.** This may necessitate the assistance of a member of your support network (discussed further below) or a professional. Throwing out the abuser's belongings may not be enough to move on with your life. You'll have

to live with the scars. Face everything that has happened and everything that has been taken away and ground yourself in healthy ways. When you can do that, you're truly ready to let go.

10. **Create a list.** If the narcissistic abuser continues to contact you or begins stalking you, keep a record of everything. This information will be useful if you need to obtain a no-contact order or file charges. Stalking is not only illegal, but it also violates a person's basic human rights.

11. **Describe what happened to you**. This and the previous point are closely related. Many people never report their abuse to the authorities or even their primary healthcare provider. If you are concerned about aggravating the situation, the doctor can at least refer you to resources that can assist you. These are some of the things we don't always consider when ending a toxic relationship and separating from the abuser. It's critical to remember to defend yourself from all sides so that the other person has no cards. They've clung to them for far too long. It's time for them to show their cards and pay their dues.

Making a Recovery Strategy

Before diving in and developing a recovery plan, it may be beneficial to be aware of a few facts about the recovery process that few others are aware of, or are aware of but will not tell you. These are important points to bring up so that the reason for developing your recovery plan makes more sense.

- **There isn't a set of steps to recovery.** There are no set steps for recovering from an abusive relationship, unlike recovering from substance abuse or another addiction. Recovery does not always take place in sequential steps, nor is it always linear. There's also no emphasis on specific steps, which could lead people to believe they're doing what they should be doing at the right time. Abuse can take a long time to heal, so give yourself plenty of time.

- **Social media stokes the fire**. There are some helpful platforms available, and it can be reassuring to read others' words of wisdom and personal experiences. Rather than listening to random posts from strangers, seek outposts from professionals who have knowledge, training, and experience in narcissistic abuse.
- **Learn to believe in yourself**. The mind games you were subjected to may have caused you to question your own sanity. To begin the healing process, you must learn to trust yourself again. Reestablishing your self-worth, self-esteem, and confidence—one baby step at a time—will assist you in gradually removing the negative tapes that play in your head.
- **You may never feel satisfied**. Closure represents the end of a situation, event, or experience for many of us, allowing us to simply let go. Closure can occur in a variety of ways, depending on the individual. Those attempting to start a new life after a crushingly abusive relationship with a narcissist may simply want confirmation that everything that happened wasn't their fault. Victims expect the abuser to express regret for what they went through, which a narcissist will not do. That means seeking closure in a different way, one that comes from within. The strength and courage required to remove yourself from that level of abuse is impressive, and it is not a move that many others in the same situation can make. That, as well as knowing that you ended a highly toxic relationship on your own and created a

better version of yourself, can provide you with the closure you seek. That is something the narcissist will never be able to take away from you. Accept the right assistance.

- **Embrace the right help:** It is critical to surround yourself with people who will help you recover. That means being open with your healthcare provider so they can guide you to proper body healing. You must find a therapist who is familiar with and understands the narcissistic personality and its impact on others. Unfortunately, there aren't many therapists who specialize in victims of narcissistic abuse. If you can't find one with this focus, look for one recommended by your healthcare provider, other survivors of this type of abuse, therapists who deal with the ongoing symptoms you're experiencing (e.g., anxiety, depression, PTSD), or even a therapist who specializes in cognitive behavioral therapy (CBT) or trauma-informed therapy. Both help people work through their trauma symptoms by teaching them better reactions to triggers.

We'll go over the last point in greater detail in the following chapter, but these are crucial steps in developing your personal recovery plan. There are four steps to making a template for your recovery plan, which you can change and add to as your healing goes on. Each person's perspective on their plan will be as unique as their situation, but it will include the following basic sections:

First and foremost, cut the narcissist's umbilical cord.
Some of you may have already completed this step, but it is included for those who haven't.

- Get out of denial and accept that what you're going through is abuse.
- Learn everything you can about the narcissistic personality type and arm yourself with knowledge. That gives you some control back.
- Cut off all contact and communication with the narcissist. Learn low-contact strategies if this isn't possible because the person is a family member or coworker.

Step Two: Self-Care Is Priority #1:
When in a relationship with a narcissist, the first thing to go is self-care (nurturing physical, mental, emotional, and spiritual health). This needs to be reinstated:

- Change your thinking from "They want me to __," or "I'll pay for it if I don't __," to "I need to __ for me." It will be difficult at first to prioritize yourself, but that is what self-care is all about.
- Make a strong support network of professionals, trusted family members, and friends who will help you get better.
- Reconnect with your entire self by nurturing each aspect of your overall health.
- Determine who triggers memories or emotional vulnerability and limit your contact with them.

Step Three: Check-Ins with Your Inner Self on a Daily Basis
The goal of this step is to keep your end goal in mind, ensuring that your perception of the world matches what you're doing to strengthen your inner self:

- Face every situation with integrity, accountability, and bravery.
- Perform a daily self-check to ensure that your thoughts, feelings, reactions, and behaviors are

on track. If something isn't right, consider it your daily challenge to confront and resolve.

- Perform a separate self-check whenever you come across someone who either reminds you of your abusive relationship or is toxic in some way.

Step 4: Improve Your Connection with Your Inner Self

These are the points at which you should keep everything you've done up to this point in order to keep track of what's working and what needs to be tweaked:

- Forgive yourself to release feelings of shame, guilt, or blame.
- You did everything you thought was necessary to protect yourself, and you still are.
- Allow yourself to grieve the relationship and learn to let go of all hurt feelings. This may seem strange to some, but you did spend a significant amount of time with someone and gave your heart to them. So, even if it was abusive, grief must be dealt with grief for what you gave up of yourself, grief for time lost to the abuser, or grief in whatever form it takes for you. Examine it, accept it, feel it, and then let it go.
- Maintain contact with your inner voice and ensure that everything it tells you is positive, loving, and inspiring. When it begins to play more negative tapes, remind yourself of all the good you're doing and that those tapes can no longer affect you.
- Constantly examine your limits. Are they precise enough? Is it necessary to restructure them? Do you require replacements? Have you gotten rid of the old ones that no longer serve you? Boundaries are critical for both what you accept

as appropriate from others and what they are allowed to do to you. You left a relationship where boundaries weren't respected or even acknowledged, so set and keep them right away.

- Under no circumstances should you accept any form of toxicity in your new life. You don't need to be enticed back into a world you abandoned because it hurt you.

In a nutshell, that is the recovery plan template. It may be beneficial to keep a journal or two to track your progress or to write down thoughts or feelings. These things must go somewhere, which is why therapy is beneficial. However, journaling is a cleansing and safe way to put those thoughts, concerns, and emotions somewhere, so they don't become maladaptive coping mechanisms.

In the next chapter, we'll talk about how important it is to build a strong network of support, how to rebuild your inner self, and how to incorporate a "mental toughness" mindset into your healing journey.

Negative people

CHAPTER 5

STRENGTHENING THE INNER SELF

It's natural to have questions at this point in the healing process as a thought occurs to you or as you experience a moment of weakness when you're not sure you'll make it. The most pressing question is, "How am I supposed to rebuild the person I was before meeting my narcissistic abuser when I don't remember that person?"

It's a poignant and heartbreaking question. However, believe it or not, having such inquiries indicates that you are on the path to healing and are unaware of it. You were always the person you were before your abuser entered your life. They were simply pushed aside and ignored while you attended to the needs of the narcissist. By asking the above question or any of the others that may be on your mind (which we'll address shortly), you're indicating that your inner self wants to be heard again. Now that another person's voice isn't occupying every space in your head, your own needs are rising to the surface. So, you can rebuild the person you once were. You simply need to construct them on a stronger foundation. This is the focus of this chapter.

First, we'll discuss the stages of recovery from narcissistic abuse. Allow yourself to go through these so that everything is acknowledged and addressed in the healthiest way possible. If any loose threads are not addressed, a single tug will unravel all your hard work. There are things you must do (and not do) within these stages to solidify your recovery and healing path.

The second area to investigate is developing your support networks. There are five different types of support networks to build because your needs differ slightly from those in each group. These are the people to whom you may need to reach out during and after your decision to leave your abusive relationship. Some of those people may have been present prior to and during the experience. Others may have provided you with information or insight that allowed you to see the light of change. We'll discuss how to put them together, who to include and who not to include, and why their presence is critical to your healing and recovery.

Healing Stages and the Importance of Support Networks

It's normal to go through different stages of recovery and healing, and it's also normal to move back and forth through stages as old feelings surface and need to be addressed. There are no hard-and-fast rules for how to recover or how long it should take You are already in the first stage, actively deciding to heal.

It could be the result of a single event—the straw that broke the camel's back—or an epiphany when you realize enough is enough. In any case, you were sick of feeling bad all the time and knew you had to do something about it. It's not uncommon to feel stuck at this stage because recognizing a problem and taking action to effect change are two distinct stages. When you realize you need to feel better, you progress to the next set of stages:

- **Getting rid of all toxins**. This isn't just about getting rid of the narcissist; it's also about getting rid of all the negativity they instilled in you. That needs to be outside of you and far away from you. It entails putting yourself in the shoes of the abuser and viewing the world through their eyes. You've been doing this by learning everything you can about narcissism and understanding who these people are and how they operate. This isn't meant to elicit empathy for them but rather to demonstrate how they were able to get you to absorb their negativity in order for you to purge the toxicity from your body and mind. Their words will not vanish instantly, or even at all in some cases. This is a difficult but necessary step that will bring you closer to healing.

- **Anxiety management**. "Well, there you go! "The most difficult part is over!" This is not correct. The difficult part at first is that there is nothing else to distract you from the chaos. Consider this: Someone has been constantly on you, putting you down, making you question everything you do, criticizing you, and causing crippling anxiety. It can be difficult to adjust to having only you to think about after not being a consideration for so long. In fact, it can exacerbate anxiety. Reaching out to support groups or those in your personal support network comes in handy at this point. Don't be afraid to seek professional assistance as well. This is not the time to try to handle everything on your own.

- **Become enraged.** Every recovery or healing plan includes a stage in which you must allow yourself to feel every emotion you experience. Anger is a common emotion. Be angry at the abuser for what they did to you; be angry for not seeing it or dealing with it when you did; be angry for how many ways they infected you; and be angry that you're the one still suffering when they may have moved on with their lives guilt-free. This stage may pass through other stages, which is fine. It means you've won. **Accept the truth to forgive yourself.** This could also be a difficult stage to get through. After all, how can you forgive yourself for putting yourself in that situation and continuing to associate with the toxic person? That is why you must. The narcissist did and said horrible things that made everything your fault. They did this so frequently and so intensely that you internalized the undeserved accountability. By forgiving yourself, you are combating that mindset by saying, "It wasn't my fault. Nothing went wrong with me." I had no idea what I was doing." This will prevent self-blame, shame, or guilt from creeping back in and distracting you from your healing. Forgiveness is a powerful act, especially when it is extended to oneself.

- **Set and follow the no-contact rule**. This was discussed earlier, but the no-contact boundary you established when you left must remain unbroken and uncrossed from either side. Do everything you can—everything humanly possible—to resist their entreaties to return. They are not going to change. Losing you has taught them nothing. You are not accountable for them. It could get nasty. They might even go behind your back and try to make you look bad. Allow them. They are the ones who look bad when you aren't fighting back or retaliating. Stay focused on your path.

- **Don't jump into a new relationship too quickly**. Getting involved with a new person while you're recovering from an abusive relationship isn't healthy for either of you. You must still deal with everything that has happened to you, and you may still be in a vulnerable state to attract another narcissist. Allow yourself time to heal before re-entering the pool.

- **Accept your new life and let go.** This will take a long time to come to an honest and complete conclusion, but it will. Allow yourself the necessary time to forgive yourself and replenish your soul with all the strength, beauty, and light it has been lacking. Continue on in your new life until you are able to let go and finally have peace.

As you progress through each of these stages, you need to know that help is available to you whenever you need it. This is a time in your life when you must reach out, accept, and embrace any offers of help from trusted individuals.

There are some things in life that you should not have to face alone.

The lowdown on personal support networks
As is probably becoming clear, there are several factors involved in successfully recovering—one of which is having a strong support network comprised of friends, fellow survivors, faith confidantes, friends, family, and therapists. The number of people who support you isn't as important as the unconditional, loving support they can provide. Not only does this support improve mental health, but it can also help you get through difficult or weak times and alleviate feelings of isolation or loneliness.

Social networks, in particular, provide the healing properties we lacked while with someone who had no connection to such behaviors and emotions as being cared for and about and being valued for who we are. These networks are divided into four categories based on what we use them for:

- **Appraisal:** We turn to those in this branch of the support network for reminders of our strengths and attributes. They also assist us in maintaining our sense of self-worth, self-esteem, and confidence.
- **Informational:** These network members are those who are familiar with dealing with stressful situations or specific issues, as well as where to find resources, insight, or additional assistance.

- **Instrumental:** Also known as tangible, these are people to whom we can turn for specific services such as a ride to an appointment, picking up a few items at the store, or even providing financial assistance when needed. These acts of kindness are from the heart, unconditional, and with no expectation of ". You require it, and they assist you.
- **Emotional:** Of all support networks, those that provide emotional support may be the most needed. These are your huggers, tear wipers, steely shoulders, and ongoing nurturing. They'd be the people who don't need to say anything. They understand that sometimes just being present is enough.

Whatever the narcissistic ex does during the breakup, certain people will always be there for us. When one person slams another and that person does not retaliate in any way, it says more about the person slamming than it does about the person being slammed. More importantly, even if you don't say anything, there will be those who can see what you're going through, and these are the supporters who will turn a deaf ear to the abuser. However, it never hurts to refresh your network on a regular basis. There will be those you expect to see but don't. There are those who would attend, but they may be dealing with personal issues that require their attention. What you're going through right now may necessitate reaching out to a different set of resources than you had previously. You may be wondering, however, how, to whom, and where you should reach out. Then there are the aftereffects of being in an abusive relationship, which have harmed your trust in others and in yourself. It may be reassuring to remember that there are many other people dealing with the aftereffects of trauma; they just need safe and approachable ways to connect with one another. One important point to emphasize here is to exercise caution when casting your social net. We tend to attract people based on the vibe we emit. When we look for people who have been in a narcissistic or abusive relationship, one of two things can happen. You'd either attract people who are in the same place as you, which isn't necessarily a bad thing—unless they unintentionally keep you there. When you have other survivors in your network, your goal should be to embrace those who have been where you are and made it to the end. These are the people you want to be once you've completed your recovery and healing journey. Connecting with someone who hasn't fully reached that point is akin to two people struggling to keep their heads above water while trying to keep each other afloat. The point is that if someone requires as much support as you do, or even more, they aren't someone to approach just yet. Another possibility is that you will attract another narcissist. They appear to be aware of when a person is at their most vulnerable to move in. This could be someone you don't notice right away because you haven't fully recovered from the previous toxic relationship. However, you have an advantage in that you are more knowledgeable and aware than you were previously, so if things start to feel familiar, run.

With that said, here are a few risk-free ways to try to broaden your social network:

- **Obtain a pet.** Having a furry friend has numerous advantages on its own. They are devoted companions who expect nothing but love and attention (and return it), and they give you a reason to stay healthy and keep going. You can also meet other pet owners if you go to the dog park.
- **Find a hobby.** This could be one you saved from a previous relationship or something brand new you've always been interested in but never tried. Investigate whether there are small groups in your community where you can paint, sculpt, or even take up a sporty hobby. You will not only be expanding your mind and keeping it busy in a healthy way, but you will also meet others who share your interests.
- **Connect via the internet.** There are numerous Facebook, Instagram, and other social media groups, as well as online groups established by community therapists. Modern technology makes it much easier to stay connected, especially when you don't feel well enough to leave your house. Be cautious online once more, as there are many predators on the world wide web.
- **Become a volunteer.** This is an excellent way to boost your self-esteem and self-worth by assisting others in some way. A word of caution here those in desperate need may be drawn to those in desperate need, even if you don't think you give off that vibe. Just don't help or give at your own expense.

- **Reconnect with those who are already part of your network**. You know they are your most dependable and loyal supporters in times of need but try contacting them just to talk or hang out when there is no trauma involved. Take them out to lunch or coffee, invite them over to watch a show or movie, or even take them for a walk or mini adventure. These are important times for the supporter as well as for you because, trauma aside, they are your friends and family, and you value them.

Adopting a mentally tough mindset to stay on track. Some of the most successful people adopt a mentally tough attitude. Given that your mental health was the most damaged aspect of you during your narcissistic, abusive relationship, finding the best way to heal it is critical. Being mentally tough has nothing to do with arrogance or ego. It's more about being well-equipped to face adversity with a "get up, dust off, and keep going" attitude. And you absolutely can do it. Mental toughness is a component of your inner self that provides you with the courage and strength to stick to your life plan and achieve your goal. And when you hit a snag, you see it as a challenge to overcome rather than a mountain of defeat. This isn't a quality that victims are encouraged to develop during their healing process, but adopting a mentally tough mindset will help you keep going up the steps we've discussed throughout this book.

Here are some of the most common methods for developing mental toughness:

- **They are thankful**. To keep things in perspective, they concentrate on the good things in their lives rather than dwelling on the bad.

- **They keep their power close at hand.** This is an important one to remember after having it taken away from you in your toxic relationship. Mentally tough people learn not to let negative people steal their power, and they don't blame others for their limitations.

- **They only concentrate on what they can control. This** is also a critical point for victims. When you are mentally tough, you only have control over what you can control. Worrying about things over which you have no control causes unnecessary stress and anxiety. Take care of what is in front of you and let the rest go.

- **They have clear boundaries**. We've talked about how important boundaries are. Mentally tough people refuse to let others push their boundaries and have no problem saying no.

- **They aren't afraid to take calculated risks.** A mentally tough person understands that it's healthy to take logical, calculated risks to better themselves, just as you were brave enough to get away from your former abuser or each time you let your guard down a tiny bit to allow someone else in.

- **Their past has no bearing on their present or future.** It's good to know the past exists, but it's not good to let it seep into your present. Don't dwell on the past; instead, let go of grudges and use them as a source of strength rather than an excuse to not move forward.

- **They regard mistakes as learning xperiences.** We're humans, and we make mistakes, but we can't punish ourselves for every poor decision or error. Consider them an opportunity to learn new skills.

- **They make no comparisons to others**. We're all individuals with different interests and goals.

That means our definitions of success are also different. By making the decision to leave your abuser, you achieved tremendous success. That is something to be proud of, and it is evidence of your success.

- **They are capable of being alone at times.** As we previously discussed, being alone after leaving an abusive relationship can be terrifying. But, in time, you'll appreciate alone time because it allows you to recharge your batteries, reflect on current events in your life, or do some soul-searching.
- **They are tenacious.** This essentially means that mentally tough individuals do not give up easily. They understand that the most important things in life, such as your complete healing, can take time. They practice patience and perseverance even when the odds appear to be stacked against them.
- **They are aware of how their beliefs affect them.** As you are aware, the inner dialogue we use can either help or hinder us. You, like mentally tough people, must be aware of the negative beliefs that keep you from getting where you want to go.
- **They adhere to their values.** This revolves around your priorities and sticking to them, even if they are not the most popular in the eyes of others. Your values and beliefs work in tandem, and you should always be brave enough to stick to them.
- **They practice being optimistic.** This is an important point to remember because leaving an abusive relationship can leave you feeling rather pessimistic about your future. The key is to maintain a realistic optimism in which you do not listen to the pessimistic voice but do not

allow yourself to become overconfident and set yourself up for failure.

- **They put up with unpleasantness**: This means that if you reach a little bit beyond your comfort zone and feel a little uncomfortable, try moving through it. It's a way to build self-discipline and know that you'll be fine going out once in a while, despite everything you've been through.

Many of these characteristics you probably already have but aren't aware of.Weave the characteristics of a mentally tough person into your strategy, and you'll notice your inner self becoming stronger with each challenge.

In our final chapter, we'll compile all of the tips and strategies to help you navigate the rest of your healing journey using a holistic approach.

CHAPTER 6

PUTTING IT ALL TOGETHER

You've learned a variety of techniques for recognizing that you're in a narcissistic, abusive relationship. You learned how to fortify your inner self in order to exit the relationship and devise a plan of action to begin your recovery and healing. Now we're going to put everything together to make sure you stay on track. The goal of this chapter is to get you ready to go from here.

You'll learn more ways to make sure that the relationships you have from now on are healthy, respectful, and loving. You've already gotten half way there by reconnecting with the inner self you'd forgotten about while with your narcissistic abuser. The key is to keep that self-visible, reminding you of all the good in you that is worth fighting for, which means breaking the narcissist relationship cycle. Another point to emphasize is the importance of living a more mindful life.

The foundation of this viewpoint is to acknowledge the past while not allowing it to infiltrate your present. It also entails visualizing your future without looking so far ahead that you lose control of the present. The overall perception is to live each day to the fullest while understanding that the past is only a part of who we are and that the future will bring us what we need to experience to guide us to where we need to be. Lastly, we'll talk about some holistic ways to add to your list of resources that can help you live more mindfully.

The holistic approach maintains the body, mind, and spirit views and treats the body as a whole rather than individual components. The suggested practices are ways to fortify your inner self and inspire you not to let another person drain it again.

Putting an End to the Narcissistic Relationship Abuse Cycle

The main takeaway from being free of a narcissistic relationship is that there are two people in the relationship, and the only one over whom you have control is you. It's frustrating to realize that the trait that drew a narcissist to us is that we are sensitive, caring, and empathetic people. These are traits they lack and desperately desire, and they inappropriately drain others of them. On the other hand, we are people who enjoy taking care of others, so the narcissist benefits everyone.

Being sensitive to the needs of others is not a bad thing. But it's a problem when it's at your own expense and becomes an obvious unfulfilled need. Simply telling yourself that you will not allow it to happen again is insufficient. Kindness and nurturing are in your nature, and you should not have to change that valuable trait because others take advantage of it. Simply put, you need to stop trying so hard to please others and figure out what you want out of a relationship that you aren't getting.

This is the source of maladaptive relationship patterns. To stop attracting toxic people who will only take advantage of your beautiful qualities, you must first understand what you want and need. Only then will you be able to trust yourself enough to allow only those close to you who respect your definition of acceptable and unacceptable treatment to treat you. Here are some questions to consider:

- **What are my requirements?** Are you putting so much effort into caring for and assisting others because you didn't get enough of it yourself? What unmet need are you attempting to fill by prioritizing other people's wants over your own? These are difficult questions to answer, but if you're assisting others to fulfill their wants rather than their needs, you're not doing it for the right reasons. To be honest, never give at your own expense.

- **Have I stated my requirements clearly**? Are you aware of your own needs? You should be able to express your needs as well as your emotions. If the other person in the relationship either does not acknowledge or does not appear to care about your needs, this is the first sign that you're on another toxic path.

- **Are you assisting the other person more than they are attempting to assist themselves?** This is truly eye-opening. If you've made things so easy for the other person that they're not even trying to do things for themselves, you need to stop. Relationships are about giving and taking, and if the other person is only taking, they should leave.

- **Did you make it clear what you expected?** If you've stated your requirements, have you also stated your expectations? When you express your needs, but the other person makes no effort to meet them, they are failing to meet your expectations. We all have the right to have our basic needs met in any relationship, and if the other person isn't upholding their end of the bargain, they don't deserve you.

- **Are your needs and feelings still being ignored after you've tried everything**? In a nutshell, if you've done everything you can to help them understand your point of view and they're still not interested, move on. Don't waste another moment with someone who is only concerned with their own wants and needs.

Adopting this mindset will alter your perception of others and lead to the formation of healthier relationships. You'll grow into a person who won't accept anything less than the absolute best for you, and those who value those characteristics will get ahead of those who don't.

For good, stop attracting narcissists.

Now that your needs are clear and you know how to ensure they are, we'll move on to the other components that will keep you from getting into another narcissistic, abusive relationship. Aside from what was discussed in the previous section, there are five additional factors to consider when attempting to solve the puzzle of being unable to ward off narcissists:

- **Did you grow up with a narcissistic parent?** The first thing to consider is whether this behavior is genetic or learned. However, there is some justification for considering what you learned from your caregivers or even other family members. You've learned about the characteristics of a narcissist. The question is, do you notice any of these characteristics in either of your caregivers, other family members, friends, or a different ex? If this is the case, you may be drawn to the same toxic relationships because they are familiar to you. Even when it is the most maladaptive, the familiar is more comfortable than trying something new.

- **Are you extremely sensitive to the emotions of others?** This is empathy, which, as previously stated, is a fantastic trait. However, narcissists seek out this trait in their partners and relish taking advantage of their emotional generosity. Those people will never appreciate that quality in you, so waiting for gratitude will never be fulfilled.

- **Do you struggle with low self-esteem**? The irony is that some narcissists actually attach themselves to other narcissists, or at least those with stronger personalities, so they can reap the benefits without putting in any effort. Those with low self-esteem, on the other hand, are much easier to manipulate and exploit, as well as to control. We've provided numerous strategies for increasing your self-esteem and using it as a deterrent against toxic narcissists.

- **Do you stifle your own desires?** This was covered in detail in the previous section, but it bears repeating. When dealing with a narcissist, denying yourself your needs puts you in a very dangerous position. They expect you to prioritize them and their needs, so denying or ignoring your own needs for theirs gives them exactly what they want: a partner who has no emotional needs and can focus solely on them. When the toxic person perceives you in this light, they will make it even more difficult for you to leave.

There are several other questions you can ask yourself, but you've most likely gotten to the point where you know how to break the cycle.

Here are a few reminders:

1. **Establish those boundaries**. This is a point we've brought up several times throughout the book, but it's critical to remember. Your boundaries are your self-imposed rules that prevent others from abusing, exploiting, or otherwise mistreating you.Know what you will and will not accept, set boundaries that honor those things, and then stand firm behind them.
2. **Increase your self-esteem**. Your self-esteem and confidence are Confidence is our belief in our abilities and what we can accomplish, whereas self-esteem is our belief in ourselves and what confidence requires to progress. Narcissists prefer partners who are low in both areas because they are easier to inextricably linked. manipulate, control, and exploit. A narcissist will lose interest in someone who cannot be used to their advantage.
3. **Make values a priority in your life**. A narcissist can't pretend to understand or connect with something they don't understand or connect with, so specify your values and morals, then try to get them to open about theirs. Understanding these things necessitates empathy and the ability to see situations through the eyes of others.

Knowing that those things are important to you, you will quickly turn them off.

4. **Be wary of red flags**. You already know who the narcissist is and what his or her most prominent personality traits are. You'd think that after being involved with them and now being away from them, you'd recognize another one from a mile away. They can slip under your highly sensitive radar because they are deceptive people. They understand how to act differently in different situations, particularly when it comes to their treatment of their intimate partner. When a relationship is healthy, there is no indication that something is wrong. Remember that your gut instincts are usually correct, so if something doesn't feel quite right, it probably isn't.

5. **Only you have control over your behavior**. When someone tries to control what you do, is overly generous with their opinions, or becomes irritated when you don't do what they tell you to, this screams narcissistic tactics that you should avoid. A person who wants to be with you would respect and support you for who you are and how you choose to be.

Rather than viewing this as a traumatic event in your past, consider it a challenge that enabled you to become an expert on the narcissistic personality. From that chaos arose your expanded perspective on everything you want and need for yourself, including everything you embrace and also let go.

Mindfulness Will Help You Live the Rest of Your Toxic-Free Life

One aspect we discussed earlier is how beneficial it is for your overall healing to live mindfully. This is the ability to become aware of your entire self—physically, mentally, and spiritually—and to accept the present moment for all it's worth. This mindset is especially beneficial for those who worry, are anxious, are depressed, or have experienced trauma, which is why it could be an invaluable strategy to incorporate into your new life plan Because the road to recovery and healing is frequently bumpy and turbulent, with periods of taking a few steps back, mindfulness helps to bring us back to the present and make us more aware of everything around us. It teaches us that life is full of gifts for which we should be grateful and that living each day to the fullest makes life meaningful. Mindfulness is not a goal but rather a point of view to adopt, and there are a few techniques to try in order to practice mindfulness:

- **Restructure our self-destructive thoughts**. What has happened to you should not define who you are. We are our harshest critics, and as we learned from being in a toxic relationship, negative talk is much easier to believe than positive talk. Turn those cutting, negative thoughts into more positive and uplifting words every time they arise.
- **Teach yourself how to relax once more**. You're on edge with a narcissistic partner, waiting for their beck and call and dealing with their high wants and needs. Keeping the body in this state all the time is extremely harmful. One good strategy is to be aware of toxic, negative energy when it arises and demands your attention, and then... stop. Don't respond right away. Instead, sit still and become more aware of that demand circling in your head, then imagine yourself pulling away from it or pushing it out of the way. Sit in this position for a few minutes, or until you can move on to something else.

- **Be mindful of your breathing**. The act of breathing is much more than simply providing the body with the oxygen it requires. It's an effective way to re-channel your response and behavior when confronted with negativity or diversity. Deep breathing is beneficial to your overall health and relaxes you, allowing you to better channel your emotions. Deliberate and deep breathing is also a key component of meditation, which is a great way to process thoughts and emotions before they explode. You'll find meaning in everything you do once you've calmed down.

- **Keeping a journal** Keeping a journal can help you channel your thoughts, emotions, or whatever else is affecting your overall mental function. Setting aside time each day to write down whatever is on your mind at the time is therapeutic and a very safe way to express yourself. When you go over what you've written, you'll be able to see what's bothering you and why, and you'll be able to take appropriate action to get things back on track.

The aftereffects of ending a narcissistic and abusive relationship can last a long time. Even if we successfully overcome all of the triggers, periods of self-doubt, and moments of weakness wondering if we made the right decision to leave, there will be times when we revert to those terrible times that nearly destroyed us. There may even be a temptation to resort to maladaptive coping strategies in order to silence those whispers from the past. Here's an analogy to remember during those times:

Consider your past to be a glass wall. You can see it happening right there, but it can't get to you because of that wall. The issue is that the wall should be behind you rather than in front of you, informing your every thought. What lies ahead of you is your future, which has not yet occurred.

And you can't let it share the present with you because there isn't enough space for both of you. It's extremely difficult not to allow it to exist because it can be so strong and powerful. But, as you progress through each baby step of your healing and recovery plan, that glass wall will gradually shift to where it belongs: behind you. You are permitted to revisit it on occasion. After all, what's behind that glass wall contributed to your current situation. It loses its power once it settles behind you, and you'll know you've made it through at that point. That is the primary reason for living life mindfully and in the present moment. You must be fully aware of your immediate surroundings and make them safe from any invasion by your trauma behind that glass wall, as well as know how to accept things as they are today, in order to live the rest of your life in inner peace.

Conclusion

We stated at the outset of this book that the emphasis is not on bringing empathy for the narcissists with whom we share the world but rather on their victims who blindly enter into relationships with them Although we covered the fundamentals of what a narcissist is, the reasons they became that way, and the most common tactics they use on their partners, The main focus is on providing insight, strategies, and tips to those who have left a narcissistic or abusiverelationship.

The difficulties you faced back then, as well as the perseverance required to stay on your healing path, will not end when you close this book. The points and pearls of wisdom will be here to review, to uplift you, to remind you of all the good you're doing, and to be a silent cheerleader that will remain with you until "I'm healing" becomes "I'm healed.".At the end of this book, we'll provide a list of various holistic therapies that you can look into. These practices are included as extra resources to help you stay grounded and focused as you celebrate your new life path. They adhere to the book's recurring theme of treating the whole person, not just the separate components of body, mind, and spirit. Remember to consult your primary health care provider before beginning any type of therapy, whether holistic or traditional.

They will know which methods will provide you with the most benefits or which combination of practices will work best for you. That is a precaution that should not be taken lightly. As a final round of applause, we'll share lessons we hope you've learned since leaving the toxic relationship and having the courage to want better for yourself. You should be proud of everything you've accomplished because there are those who are still where you were. Perhaps one day you will be able to use all of your knowledge to advocate for those whose voices are drowned out by the one speaking over them.

That is extremely effective. We stated at the outset of this book that the emphasis is not on bringing empathy for the narcissists with whom we share the world but rather on their victims who blindly enter into relationships with them. Although we covered the fundamentals of what a narcissist is, the reasons they became that way, and the most common tactics they use on their partners, The main focus is on providing insight, strategies, and tips to those who have left a narcissistic or abusive relationship. The difficulties you faced back then, as well as the perseverance required to stay on your healing path, will not end when you close this book. The points and pearls of wisdom will be here to review, to uplift you, to remind you of all the good you're doing, and to be a silent cheerleader that will remain with you until "I'm healing" becomes "I'm healed.".

At the end of this book, we'll provide a list of various holistic therapies that you can look into. These practices are included as extra resources to help you stay grounded and focused as you celebrate your new life path. They adhere to the book's recurring theme of treating the whole person, not just the separate components of body, mind, and spirit. Remember to consult your primary health care provider before beginning any type of therapy, whether holistic or traditional.

They will know which methods will provide you with the most benefits or which combination of practices will work best for you. That is a precaution that should not be taken lightly. As a final round of applause, we'll share lessons we hope you've learned since leaving the toxic relationship and having the courage to want better for yourself. You should be proud of everything you've accomplished because there are those who are still where you were. Perhaps one day you will be able to use all your knowledge to advocate for those whose voices are drowned out by the one speaking over them. That is extremely effective.

CHAPTER 7

HOLISTIC PRACTICES FOR GENERAL HEALTH 101

Holistic therapy is good for anyone who wants to be as healthy as possible, but it is especially good for people with anxiety, depression, high stress, or trauma. All of these are mental states that throw the whole body out of whack and make it hard to act in the right way. Keeping the body in a constant state of fear, fight, or response can hurt health in many ways. There are many different types of holistic therapies, all of which aim to realign the energies in the body so that the individual can return to a resting state and help the body's energies get back in sync. The most common types of these therapies that are most effective in dealing with the body-mind-brain connection, particularly trauma, are as follows:

1. Breathwork: As being in tune with one's breathing is the foundation for many of the practices, this may be one of the first to try. It allows us to control and become more conscious of our breathing. It is beneficial to those who have experienced trauma because it helps to regulate the nervous system (e.g., heart rate, breathing, nervousness, and so on). Other advantages include increased lung capacity, reduced anxiety symptoms, and improved sleep.

2. Meditation and yoga: These practices are also beneficial to those suffering from the aftereffects of trauma. Both emphasize the significance of breathing. Meditation, on the other hand, brings

the mind back to and keeps it in the present moment, whereas yoga reconnects the mind-body-spirit through specific poses tailored to the individual's needs.

3. Stress management: The individual is guided through the process of developing a plan to deal with stress head-on rather than letting it build up. Each plan will look different for each person because our stressors, their intensity, and our tolerance level for dealing with them are all unique. However, effective stress management can significantly reduce the negative effects of stress on our overall health.

4. Somatic experiencing: This is a way for people with PTSD or other types of traumas to focus on how their bodies are reacting to the event before they deal with their mental symptoms. Many people who have been through a traumatic event have symptoms that are so bad that they can't do any other kind of therapy to deal with it.Connecting with and working through how that event made the body feel puts a person in a stronger position to deal with the trauma in a healthier way.

5. Cognitive-behavioral therapy (CBT): This practice teaches us how our thoughts and emotions influence our reactions and behaviors. The primary goal is for the individual to recognize patterns in their thoughts and emotions and then restructure them in a more positive and effective manner. It should be noted that this type of treatment focuses on how to cope better in the present rather than on past events. This is not the best type of therapy for someone who wants to get to the bottom of their behavior.

6. Acupuncture: This practice has been used in Chinese medicine for centuries to realign

disconnected energies in the body by inserting needles at specific points in the body. It has been shown to alleviate pain, anxiety, and a variety of other symptoms.

7. Chiropractic: Using a series of spinal adjustments, practitioners of this approach focus on strengthening and stimulating the brain-spine connection as well as healing physiological and emotional issues.

8. Massage has gradually become one of the more popular practices for dealing with the bodily symptoms of stress, anxiety, and trauma. When the body is under stress, the muscles become tense, and massage can help relieve pain, relieve stress, and realign disconnected energies. Tai chi practice is similar to moving through meditation. A centuries-old Chinese form of low-impact martial arts that combines the benefits of breathwork, motion, and focus.

9. Grounding: For those suffering from PTSD, traumatic memories, dissociation, or anxiety, this practice can help with flashbacks or triggers of terrifying memories by focusing the individual on the present rather than succumbing to the trigger pull of the past.

10. Cranial-sacral therapy (CST): This relieves tension and compression in the head, neck, and spine, which are common sources of stress and tension for many people. For many people, easing discomfort in these areas can help them deal with the underlying cause of their symptoms.

11. Reiki: This is a Japanese practice that focuses on realigning the body's energies as well as unblocking any blocked energy paths caused by prolonged stress and trauma.

12. Sound healing: In this method, instruments like singing bowls are used to make sounds and

vibrations. The vibrations influence brain waves and help to balance the chakra systems, which are energy centers linked to specific organs and systems in the body.

13. Guided imaging therapy (GIT): This practice focuses on positive imagery in order to return the body to a calm and relaxed state of mind in order to work through any negative thoughts or emotions that may have been ignored or repressed.

14. Emotional Freedom Technique (EFT) 15: Taping on major energy pathways, also called "mind acupuncture," helps to refocus physical symptoms, which leads to mental, emotional, and physical healing.

As you can see, you have a lot of choices, depending on your needs, how you feel about touch, and how bad your symptoms are. The holistic approach is an umbrella of practices to incorporate into your existing healing plan. To reiterate an earlier point, do not begin any practice without first obtaining permission from your primary healthcare provider.

10 Things You Discovered After Surviving Narcissistic Abuse

After everything you've been through and worked through in this book, your job should now be to focus on healing. As previously stated, you should not seek out another relationship until you are on stronger, more stable ground. However, you now have all the tools necessary to transition into a healthier relationship with someone who treats you the way you deserve to be treated.

In an odd way, the narcissist taught you a few valuable lessons. They showed you all the flaws you shouldn't tolerate while also guiding you to a clearer understanding of your needs, wants, and values, as well as your new definition of love. With that in mind, here are the ten lessons we hope you've learned since leaving your abusive, narcissistic relationship:

- False flattery does not fool you. You now understand that all of the love-bombing, attention, gifts, and other promises aren't given from the person's heart, but rather as a way to entice you to come closer and adore them. As a result, you can distinguish between genuine intentions and false flattery.
- You prefer "slow and steady" to "fast and furious." In a nutshell, a narcissist does not want to waste time getting to know each other "inside and out" before making serious plans. They want what they want right away. You immediately recognize the red flag and know that any relationship with you is worth the wait.
- Being held accountable has value. You know that a narcissist would rather see another person suffer for their mistakes than bear responsibility for their own. It takes a much more mature person to not only admit their mistakes, but also to learn from them and fix what they can.
- You understand the value of having a life outside of a relationship. You may not have recognized the value of having hobbies, interests, or even connections outside of your narcissistic relationship. They never saw the point in such things when you could focus all of your attention and energy on them. Having these things in your life allows you to focus on your needs, which you were not previously allowed to do. A new person in your life will understand and support your requirements.

- It made you stronger than you thought. You understand how difficult it is to be in a toxic relationship and how difficult it is to end it and rebuild your life. But you succeeded. The strength comes from transforming all the negatives you encountered into learning blocks from which to blossom and grow.
- You understand that a toxic relationship is not a sign of weakness. Recognizing the toxicity and removing yourself from it are, if anything, signs of strength. When you think about it, the narcissist was feeding on your strengths of empathy, kindness, and caring nature, not your weaknesses. These are qualities that a newcomer will treasure and value.
- You discovered that partners celebrate each other's accomplishments. Narcissists don't mind if their partners succeed if they don't step on their toes. They don't like it when their significant other is in the spotlight and punish them harshly for it. You now understand that a supportive partner will celebrate every accomplishment and achievement with you and will never judge you for them.
- You understand the importance of setting clear boundaries. Narcissists not only have no boundaries, but they also do not respect them. How can they be expected to respect something they don't even comprehend? After having your boundaries constantly broken and crossed, you know how important it is to set them, make sure they are strong, and make sure no one crosses them.
- You recognize that being emotionally vulnerable is a sign of strength. Showing emotions or any form of emotional vulnerability is regarded as a sign of weakness by narcissists. To be willing to

show vulnerability to another takes a much braver and stronger person. It demonstrates trust, openness, and a desire to progress in a relationship. There is no flaw in any of them.

- You realize you can't please everyone. One of the difficult lessons you learned is that narcissists are impossible to truly please, despite your best efforts. They seek perfection, which does not exist. Human beings are all flawed in some way; it is what distinguishes us. You've learned that your happiness comes first and that anyone who wants to be with you must agree with that premise, just as you would for them.

We hope you've learned strategies and tips to help you stay on your healing path. Be proud of who you are, how hard you've worked to become who you are, and how strong you are. Your life now has a new meaning.

www.ingramcontent.com/pod-product-compliance
Lightning Source LLC
LaVergne TN
LVHW011603210726
843509LV00016BA/829